Show and Tell

Ron and Rebekah Coriell

Published Under Arrangement with
Fleming H. Revell Co. by

A publication of
ASSOCIATION OF CHRISTIAN SCHOOLS INTERNATIONAL
P.O. BOX 4097, WHITTIER, CA 90607

DESERT AHEAD
LAST CHANCE
GAS

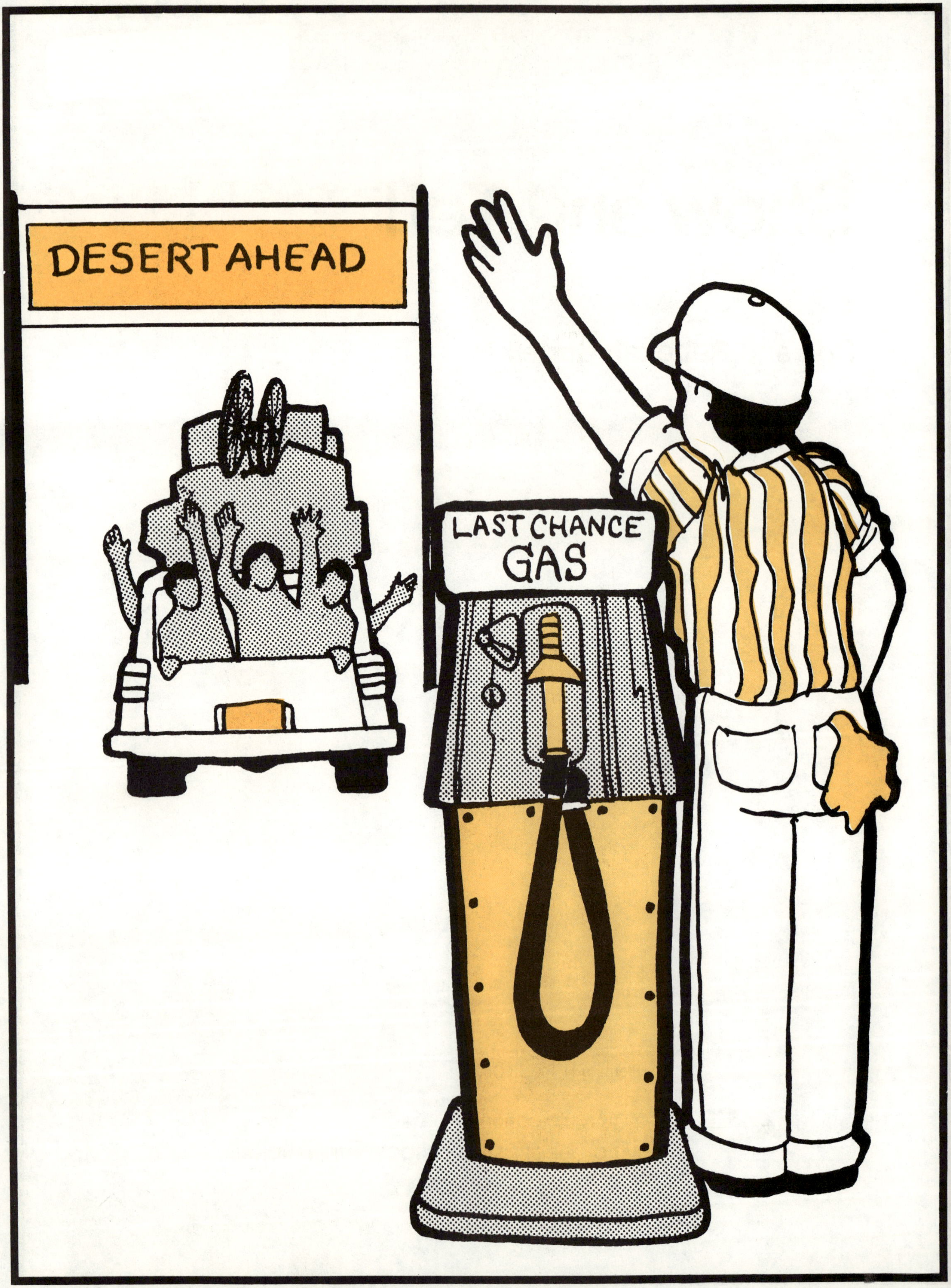

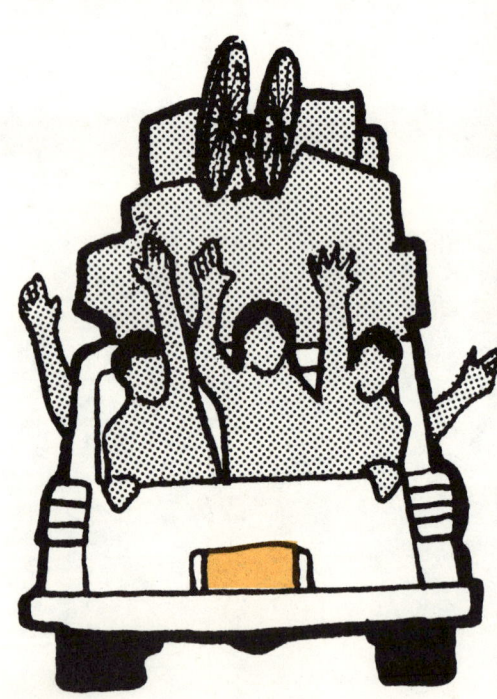

Thankful

tankful

Being Grateful and Saying So

In every thing give thanks: for this is the will of God in Christ Jesus concerning you.

1 Thessalonians 5:18

Thankfulness in the Bible

Mary of Bethany had entered the room in which Jesus and His disciples sat at dinner in Simon the leper's house. She opened an alabaster box and slowly poured its costly contents upon Jesus' head. As the smell of this perfume filled the room, Mary poured some on Jesus' feet and began to wipe them with her long hair.

The disciples of Jesus were very angry. "Why are you wasting this ointment?" Judas shouted. "Why wasn't it sold for fifty dollars and the money given to the poor?"

Jesus realized that there was deep meaning behind what Mary was doing. He said, "Let her alone. For she has done a good work for Me. For ye have the poor always with you, but you will not always have Me. She has poured this ointment on My body for My burial."

Jesus had often told His followers that He would soon die. They could not understand this, but Mary understood. The ointment she had poured on Jesus was one that people used when they buried the dead.

Gratefully, Jesus smiled as Mary finished drying His feet. He was thankful for her kindness and for her understanding. He said, "Verily I say unto you, wheresoever the gospel shall be preached, in the whole world, what this woman has done will be told as a memorial to her."

Thankfulness at Home

"Oh, no, not again," moaned Mr. Williams. "All the water in the radiator is boiling out. We can't go any farther unless we get some water."

The family sat in sadness, watching steam pour out from under the hood.

"It's getting dark, and I don't see any houses on this road. What shall we do?" asked Hank.

Reassuringly, Mother replied, "We will just have to sit and wait for help."

As the family waited, the wind began to blow, and dark clouds swirled overhead. Suddenly, Father jumped out of the car and ran back to the trunk. He lifted out an ice chest and some pots and pans. He placed them on the shoulder of the road. Heavy rain came down, just as he got back in the car. Everyone was thankful to be inside.

The storm lasted for thirty minutes. When it was over, everyone got out to inspect how well Father's idea had worked. Just as he had hoped, enough water had been collected in all the containers.

"After I fill the radiator, we'll be able to travel," Mr. Williams announced. "But, first, let's all thank God for sending us a big rainstorm. What a special way He chose to help meet our need tonight."

Thankfulness at School

"I am so tired today," sighed Hank, after school.

"Me, too," agreed Larry.

"Mrs. Clark is a good substitute teacher, but I really miss our teacher, Mrs. Mart," said Hank.

"You can say that again, Hank," responded Larry. "Remember how kind she is? She always has such a cheerful hello for everyone. She makes us feel so important. Will Mrs. Mart be back tomorrow?"

"I don't know. I learned a good lesson, while she was away, today," replied Hank.

"What lesson is that?" asked Larry.

"Well," said Hank, "we have enjoyed Mrs. Mart as a teacher. I have always been thankful for her, but I've never told her so."

With a sad look, Larry replied, "Neither have I. It is important to be grateful. And it is just as important to say you appreciate someone."

"How can we do that?" asked Hank.

"Maybe we could tell her as soon as she gets back to school," suggested Larry.

Hank thought a moment and then said, "Let's send her a get-well card. We'll tell her how thankful we are that she is our teacher. And let's say we are praying that she will get well very soon."

Thankfulness at Play

"Mother, I am so bored with these toys. I wish I had new ones," complained Hank.

"Your birthday was last month," replied Mother. "Aren't you content with the new ones that you received?"

"I like all my toys," sighed Hank, "but I am tired of them."

Mother put down her dustcloth and sat on the ottoman, in front of Hank. "Do you remember the slides we saw Sunday, at church?" she asked. "Our missionaries told us about some poor children. Do you remember that he said most of the children had to make their own toys? Do you think those children would be grateful if they had just a few of your toys?"

Hank thought a moment and answered, "I know they would be happy with even *one* of my toys. I have not been as thankful as I should be. Would Jesus understand if I asked Him to forgive me for being so ungrateful?"

"Yes, He would," assured his mother.

"And I think," said Hank, "that I had better tell Jesus, right now, how thankful I am for all the toys He has given to me."

Honesty
tree

Truthful Words and Ways

Wherefore putting away lying, speak every man truth with his neighbor. . . .

Ephesians 4:25

Honesty in the Bible

"Peter, James, John, rise up. Let us go," said Jesus.

Everything had been very quiet that Passover evening in the Garden of Gethsemane. Now the gentle hush of the trees was broken by the sounds of footsteps and rustling leaves. Lighted torches, carried by soldiers and angry men, could be seen around Jesus and His disciples. Some of the soldiers were carrying swords.

Jesus knew the mob was coming to arrest Him. It would mean suffering and death for Him. He could see Judas coming. How deeply it hurt to know that His friend was going to betray Him with a kiss. Aware of these dangers, yet unafraid, Jesus resisted any temptation to run or hide.

He faced the angry crowd. He asked, "Whom are you seeking?"

"Jesus of Nazareth," the crowd replied.

Jesus' character could only give an honest answer: "I am He." His truthful words shocked the mob so that they fell to the ground.

Again, He questioned them, "Whom are you seeking?"

"Jesus of Nazareth," the mob answered again.

"I am He. Let My disciples go," Jesus replied.

With great strength and courage, Jesus honestly faced the mob.

Honesty at Home

"Juan, now you are in big trouble," said his friend Harold. "The airplane is broken."

The boys had been playing in the den. Juan had climbed on a chair to reach a large model airplane he wanted to show Harold. It slipped out of his fingers and plunged to the floor, breaking the right wing.

Harold was afraid and asked, "Aren't you going to run?"

"Let's go," replied Juan. "Maybe Father will think the cat knocked it off."

The rest of the day, Juan's conscience bothered him. God was telling him to tell the truth about the plane. Verses of Scripture ran through his mind: ". . . be sure your sin will find you out. The eyes of the Lord are in every place beholding the evil. . . . Speak ye every man the truth. . . ."

Time passed slowly as Juan waited for his father to come home. Hearing the car in the driveway, he greeted his father at the front door. "Dad, can I talk to you alone?" asked Juan.

He led his father to the den. When Mr. Cortez saw the wrecked plane, he was surprised and disappointed.

"I dropped it, Father," said Juan. "It slipped from my fingers as I was showing it to Harold."

"I would have had a broken heart if you had not told me," said Father. "Thank you, Son, for being honest with me."

Honesty at School

"I am happy to announce that the winner of the art contest is Juan Cortez!" reported Mr. Higdon, the principal.

It can't be true, Juan thought. *I rushed to complete my picture. It can't be good enough to win.*

As Mr. Higdon shook Juan's hand, he proudly pointed to Juan's prize-winning painting. Juan's eyes grew as big as golf balls. The picture to which Mr. Higdon pointed was not his. It really belonged to Bentley Brown.

Many questions ran through Juan's mind: *What shall I do? Why was my name on the picture? How did it happen? Everyone knows Bentley is the best artist in the class. There are students in the class who do not like Bentley. I wonder if they switched my name with his, so that he wouldn't win.*

Juan had always been truthful in his words and ways. That was being like Jesus. Now he had the opportunity to show others that being honest was more important to him than winning the contest. Motioning to Mr. Higdon, he whispered the truth in the principal's ear.

"Thank you, Juan, for being so honest," said Mr. Higdon. "I will correct the mistake right now."

Juan felt a little disappointment as he handed the winner's ribbon to Bentley Brown. But he was sure that he had made the right decision. He knew he had pleased Jesus, too.

Honesty at Play

"Father, could you give me some advice?" asked Juan.

"Sure, Son," replied Mr. Cortez.

"My friend Francis is not liked by any of the neighborhood boys. It is so hard to be his friend," Juan said.

"Why don't they like Francis?" asked Father.

"The truth is," answered Juan, "that he looks and smells dirty. My friends just don't want to play with him."

"Are you being friendly to him?" his father asked.

"Sometimes, Father," said Juan. "But he must think that I would rather play with the other boys, instead of him."

"Is that true?" asked Mr. Cortez.

Embarrassed, Juan admitted, "I guess so."

Then Father tenderly lifted Juan onto his lap. He reminded him that Jesus tried to help people who were despised. He encouraged Juan to try to help Francis.

"But how?" pleaded Juan.

"By being honest and telling him the truth. In a kind way, you must tell him that being dirty makes other people unfriendly. Then pray that God will help him to change," replied Father.

The next morning, Juan was honest with Francis about his problem. Francis went home, bathed, and changed his clothes. Juan's honesty helped him make a good friend.

Joy
ahoy

**Being Happy
Inside and Out**

And my soul shall be joyful in the Lord: it shall rejoice in his salvation.

Psalms 35:9

Joyfulness in the Bible

"Go away! The Master doesn't have time for children," snapped the disciples.

Disappointedly, the mothers and fathers reached out to claim the little children they had brought to have Jesus bless. They had hoped He would place His hands on them. Instead, the disciples pushed them away.

Jesus' tender eyes saw the disappointed faces of the children and their parents. Compassionately He called, "Let the little children come to Me. Forbid them not, for of such is the kingdom of heaven."

Then, Jesus lifted up the little children in His arms and held them. It gave Him joy to know that someday He would have children of all ages with Him in heaven.

It was this joy that made Him willing to endure the cross and its shame. He could rejoice with confidence, because He was going to be obedient to death on the cross; therefore, God's children would live with Him forever.

Jesus promised the disciples that His joy would remain in them, if they obeyed God's commandments. If we obey, His joy will be in us, too.

Joyfulness at Home

Saturday was one of those days when everything seemed to go wrong. It was a test of Jenny Henson's ability to stay joyful.

Jenny got up late. She took a quick bath and dressed. Because she had trouble finding her shoes, her breakfast was cold. She gulped down her eggs and ran out the door, to catch her ride to day camp.

Although she ran all the way to the church, she was still late. When she arrived at the parking lot, she discovered that the bus had just left. Jenny wanted to cry. Her day was such a disappointment. Then her thoughts turned to Jesus and His disappointments on earth.

He was the Creator; the people He made hated Him. Lowly shepherds worshiped Him at His birth; and He was spit upon by soldiers, at His death. For three long years, He trained His disciples, only to have them run away when He was arrested.

"Jesus must surely know how I feel right now," she said aloud. "I'm not going to let my disappointing morning take away my joy."

Jenny took a deep breath and started walking home. She rejoiced as she thought that ". . . all things work together for good to them that love God, to them who are the called according to His purpose" (Romans 8:28).

Joyfulness at School

Have you ever had your heart set on something you really wanted to do? That was the way Jenny felt, in gym class. She wanted to play on the trampoline. She loved to flip in the air. Last week, she had learned to touch her toes while being in the air.

Excitedly, Jenny dressed in her gym clothes, hoping to be the first in line for the trampoline. The girls lined up as Mrs. Best, the gym teacher, blew the whistle. Then, to Jenny's surprise, Mrs. Best asked the girls to choose the game that they wanted to play. Kickball was their favorite game.

Oh, but that is not as much fun, Jenny almost shouted. *It is going to be hard to be happy playing kickball, but I will try*, she thought.

Smiling, she entered into the kickball game. Soon, her smile on the outside helped her to be happy inside, too.

When the game was over, Mrs. Best announced that Jenny's classroom teacher had to leave school early. The class would be staying in gym until school was dismissed. They could have a free period to use any of the gym equipment. As Jenny raced to the trampoline, she thought, *God sometimes has surprises for us, when we are joyful in all things.*

Joyfulness at Play

"Jenny," said her mother, "your cousin, Sally, is coming to stay with us for a month."

"Oh, that is wonderful. Now, I will have someone my age to play with," responded Jenny.

Jenny's excitement grew as the day came nearer. She had all kinds of activities planned. They would hike, swim, and catch butterflies. And they could play badminton with her new set. However, these dreams faded when her cousin was brought home from the bus station. Sally recently had been crippled in a car accident and had to walk with special braces on her legs.

Jenny smiled on the outside as she greeted Sally. On the inside, she was sad. She felt sorry for Sally and for herself. Her cousin did not let her problem make her sad. She was cheerful and ready to try anything.

As the weeks went by, with a little help, Sally joyfully swam in the pool. She hiked with Jenny, as long as they walked slowly. Sally became fairly good at catching butterflies with a net. And she could even play badminton.

Sally's cheerfulness made Jenny feel joyful, too. She never would forget her joyful cousin. And God helped Jenny to remember that it is best to have a happy spirit.

Primary Character Challenges

Here are some practical suggestions that will reinforce the concepts taught in the preceding stories.

Thankfulness

1. Encourage a child to exhibit a spirit of thankfulness by having him create an appreciation card and mail it to someone who has been kind to him.
2. Teach the child the principle of "In every thing give thanks . . ." (1 Thessalonians 5:18), by having him relate some recent, unpleasant experiences in which he had to be thankful.
3. Guide the child into developing a spirit of thankfulness by having him memorize Psalms 100:4: "Enter into his gates with thanksgiving. . . ."

Honesty

1. Being true to one's word is a valuable character trait to develop in a child. Whenever your child makes a promise, be sure to explain the importance of honesty and following through on his word.
2. Have the child memorize Ephesians 4:25 and explain its meaning.
3. Remind the child to avoid exaggeration, which is a form of dishonesty. Have him memorize Romans 12:17: ". . . Provide things honest in the sight of all men."

Joyfulness

1. John 15:10, 11 says that obedience is a key to joyfulness. Discuss with the child five ways in which he can become joyful by obeying.
2. Psalms 63:5, 6 instructs us to praise the Lord with joyful words, by meditating with Him each evening before going to sleep. Review Bible verses which speak about joy and use them at bedtime.
3. Assist the child in memorizing Philippians 2:14. Explain how the child can be joyful in what he does.